CONTENTS

03 Getting to Eritrea

05 Ethnic Group

09 Religion

11 Clothing

12 Geographical Miliues

19 Red Sea & the coastal line

23 Archaeological Sites

31 Art

35 Itinerary Railroad tour to Massawa

37 Sports

39 Music & Musical instruments

45 Itinerary visit to Asmera

51 Eritrea through out the year

54 Cuisine

59 Traditional Drinks

Copyright © 2022 All Right Reserved.

No part of this publication may be reproduced, distributed, or transmitted in any form or by any means, including photocopying, recording, or other electronic or mechanical methods, without the prior written permission of the publisher, except in the case of brief quotations embodied in critical reviews and certain other noncommercial uses permitted by copyright law. For permission requests, write to the publisher, addressed "Attention: Permissions Coordinator," at the address below.

ISBN : 9798828912612
Author : Bahran Bereket
Email : bereketbahran13@gmail.com

PREFACE

Tourism is now recognized as being an economic activity of global significance. As the importance of the activity is increasing so too has the attention given to it by governments, in both the public and private sectors. Eritrea, a magnificent country holding an interesting and amazing History, in addition to a significant geographical location in the horn of Africa, it has always a high value in the global tourism industry.

This book is written specifically for two main audiences; International tourists who want to know about Eritrea & of course for Eritreans as the information provided is mainly for Personal guide.

The author hopes to provide as much information as possible about Eritrea including getting basic services & tries to stimulate & encourage Tourists' viewpoint that there is always more for visiting the special nature & diversity of Eritrea.

As the reasons for travel could be Visiting relatives & friends, attending business & professional engagement, undertaking International, national & religious pilgrimage, or any other personal motives, this book is a gate way for all those reasons.

Owning & 30 minute reading of this book will be worth finding the pleasure a Traveler could seek.

BASIC TIGRIGNA PHRASES

Hi / hello = *selam*
Welcome = *enqa bdehan met'saka (M); enqa bdehan met'saki (F)*
Good bye = *chaw dehan kun (M); chaw dehan kuni (F)*
Thank you! = *yeqenyeley*
Please! = *bejaka(M) or bkbretka(M); bejaki (F) or bkbretki (F)*
Yes = *ewe*
No = *giega*
What's your name = *shim men kbl?*
Where is your address? = *adrasha abey yu?*
Call me! = *dewleley (M) /dewliley (F)*
Come to me = *mit'sani(M); mt'sni(F)*
How is your day = *kemey wielka (M); kemey wielki (F)*
How is your evening = *kemey amsika (M); kemey amsiki (F)*
How much is this? = *waga kindey 'yu?*
How do I get this? = *ezi kabey yrekb?*
How do I go there? = *kemey giere ykeyd?*
Where is this? = *abey yu ezi?*
What time is it? = *seat kndey alo?*
Help your self(while eating) = *niqedem belu*
Help me! = *haguzuni*
It's hot out here! = *harur alo!*
It's cold out here! = *quri alo!*

BASIC FACTS

Time zone	UTC + 3 (EAT)
Capital city	Asmera
Regions	06
Ethnics	09
Working language	Tigrinya Arabic English
Religion	Christianity (63%) Islam (36%) Others (<1%)
Demonym(s)	Eritrean
President	H.E. Isaias Afwerki
Area	117,600 km^2
Currency	Nakfa (ERN)
Population (est 2020)	6,081,196
Driving side	Right
Calling code	+291

ACKNOWLEDGEMENT

Thinking & doing are extremely different aspects. To do, anyone would need self dedication & support from possible sources. That's why nothing can be done without encouragement of the people you depend on but Firstly, I give my for most gratitude to the almighty God for keeping me safe through out my life & empower me to do such a simple yet beautiful booklet.

To my family, I have endless gratitude for they provide a wisdom for my life & shape me always to be a better person.

There goes a say "friends make the world". I can say this is my very best experience to be blessed with & enjoy a good friendship & I thank them all so much that they all are precious partners of my life.

For Eng. Amanuel Alem! From ideas to material & all kind of support, you were all over the way. This book is possible because of you & I can't thank you enough as much as I want. Thank you so much for your inspiration. Mr. Meron Mossazghi, I have been very proud to have a friend & brother as you are & I thank you so much for your all kind support. The list goes on but my special thanks goes to :-

Ms. Ariam Solomon
Mr. Yacob Habte
Eng. Robel Solomon
Eng. Samuel Tesfagabr
Eng. Kidane Estifanos
Mr. Haile Daniel
Ms. Dina Alem
Mr. Meron Naizghi
Mr. Isaias Gebray

To all who participated in making this book a reality, I offer you all my heartfelt thanks. You are living proof that other people are our greatest resource.

INTRODUCTION

Eritrea; (/ˌɛrɪˈtreɪ.ə/ or /ˌɛrɪˈtriːə/; in Tigrinya: ኤርትራ, officially The State of Eritrea, is located in the horn of Africa with it's capital Asmera, a magnificent city of Art Deco. It's a nation of Nine ethic groups with a population more than 6 Million.

The geographical creation of modern-day Eritrea is a result of the incorporation of independent, distinct kingdoms and Sultanates, eventually resulting in the formation of it's border lines in 1900 by the Italian colonizers. After the end of the Italian colonial control in 1941 and 10 years of British administrative control, the UN established Eritrea as an autonomous region within the Ethiopian federation in 1952. Ethiopia's full annexation of Eritrea as a province for 10 years forced the People to enroll a violent 30-year struggle for independence that ended in 1991 with the Eritrean people defeating the Ethiopian DURG regime. Past those difficult times, Eritreans overwhelmingly voted 99.8% for independence in a 1993 referendum. In the years after, the Economy experienced considerable growth & the country underwent extreme changes in Industries, Agriculture, Aquaculture, Animal Husbandry, manufacturing, Banking & Finance. Specially on Tourism till a two-and-a-half-year border war occurred with Ethiopia that erupted in 1998 ended in December 2000 that deterred the developments encountered by then. And with the cooperation & Hard work of the people & the Government, the overall development program has encountered significant changes led by step-by-step priorities & economical growth rate in the consecutive years.

ERITREA MAP

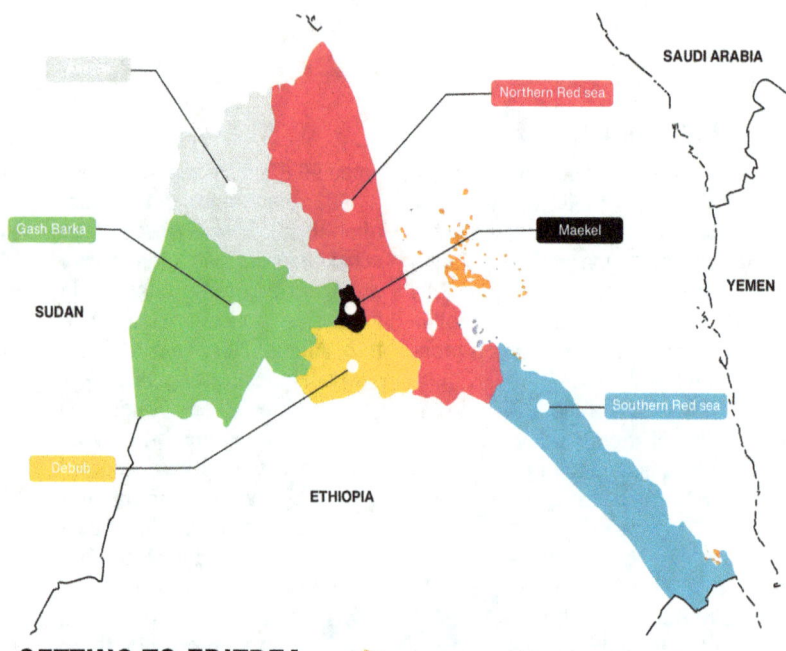

GETTING TO ERITREA

One can have several carriers to choose from, in flying to Eritrea. Obviously, Eritrean Airline serves the country the most flights, including direct flights from several remote countries & Neighboring countries as they are very close Transit Airports & You can easily find Transit flights from Dubai UAE, Addis Ababa Ethiopia, Khartoum Sudan, Juba South Sudan, Riyadh Saudi Arabia.

You can also book & use Airlines such as Fly Dubai Airline, Turkish Airline, Ethiopian Airline, Egypt Airline, Tarco Airline. Those Airlines provide non-stop flights from all over the world to Asmera International Airport and back.

GETTING AROUND

If you can afford it and you know the roads, it's highly recommended to rent a car & drive yourself. Roads are right sided with their international signs, they won't be a problem. In cities like Asmera, It's the best way to see and experience what you must visit by yourself for at least part of the trips. Particularly if you will be touring out of the main roads where there is not public bus transportation. If driving makes you nervous, you might consider hiring a guide to drive you for at least good segment of the drive until you get some awareness of the streets. This works particularly well if you have a family or a group

of three or four where the cost can be shared.
To get Assistance of Tour agencies, tour agents & Car rental services contact your guide personal. Also Inter-city Taxi will be available in all the areas you put your feet.

MONEY EXCHANGE

Eritrea's currency is the Nakfa (code : ERN) which released back in November 1997, symbolized as Nkf with a rate of $1 = 15.00 ERN. As you pay in cash when you need to buy items & use service's, you will need to change your currency in to ERN for convenience of use. It can be done easily in banks or authorized money changing shops. I suggest you don't need to carry around large sums of cash as some amount will be enough for your daily expenses.

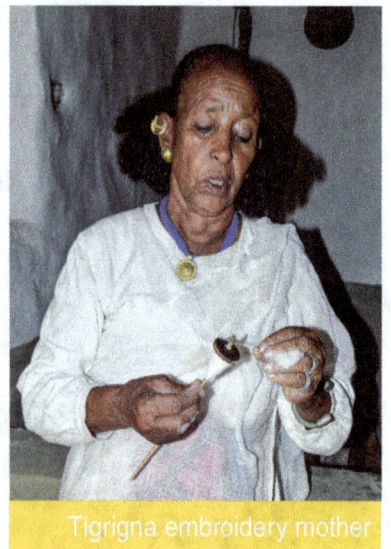
Tigrigna embroidery mother

Afar girl

Tigre bride

Hidarb man parching coffee

ETHNIC GROUP

In Eritrea there are nine ethnic groups categorized by their common ancestry. The Nilotic Nara & Kunama which forms 2% each of the current population. The Siemawyan or Arabs, Rashayda are a population of 2%. The other settlers from the Lower Kush Afar, Hidarb(Bidawyet) & Saho they each make 2%, 2% & 4% respectively. In the other hand, from the Upper Kush, the Bilen forms 2%. And the Majority the Afro-Asian Tigrigna & Tigre forms 55% & 30% of the total population.

They all have their own culture, language, & Norms of life which distinguish them from each other. Usually Members of each Ethnic group tends to share the same geographical location as Nara, kunama & Bidawyet can only be found in Western region Zoba Gash

Barka. In contrary, Afar can only be found in the Coastal cities like Assab & Massawa as for their lifestyle were dependent totally with fishing & Sea trade. In the Central Zoba Anseba mostly the Ethnic group Bilen can be found. For Tigrigna,Tigre & Saho, they can be found all around the Nation, the Ethnic group Rashayda can be located in the Northern Red Sea Zone & some around Tesseney,Gash Barka Zone.

As they were connected through times of resisting old colonizers & Armed struggle , All the people are interconnected to each other & they have an amazing Harmony of respecting their own cultural values & towards each other. As a result, the common general tradition makes them united.

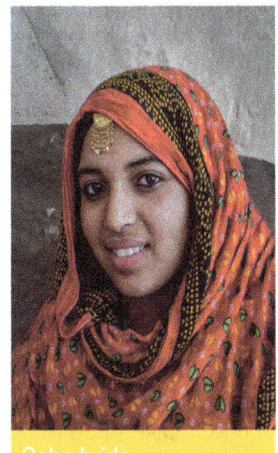
Saho bride

Bilen girl a bride to be

Kunama mother

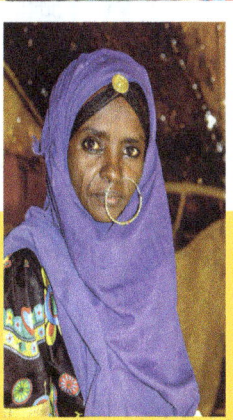
Nara mother

Rashayda woman

SECURITY ISSUES

Speaking of security, it's every ones amazement considering a peaceful, constant aspect of every Eritrean life. Despite a travelers' wondering questions, anyone is safer in Eritrea than in most major cities in Africa. Terror related incidents are never heard of, even theft isn't that much of a topic day & night. Just pay attention not to forget your belongings anywhere you go & if you do, ask for local advice to find it. As street crimes remain far too low, you really are safe & use your common sense to understand your surrounding.

LANGUAGE

In Eritrea each ethnic group have its own language & the names of their language is taken from the etymology of it user ethnic group. Although the Local languages tigrigna, arabic & the international english are the three official working language, all other local languages are widely in use & spoken among the members of the ethnic & others.

In the Eastern lowlands cities such as Gindae extending to Massawa & Assab the languages Arabic, Afar, Tigrigna,Tigre & Saho are very common.

In the Western lowland cities such as Keren,Barentu & Tesseney, the languages Bilen,Kunama,Arabic, Tigrigna,Bidawyet & Nara are widely spoken.

In the Central Highlands the languages Tigrigna,Tigre,Arabic & Saho are the native languages of the places. Although they are in low frequency, languages such as Amharic, Italian & French are widely understood among many people. In addition to this, The international Sign language is also a useful language in communicating among those who have hearing disabilities.

SOCIAL CUSTOM & NORMS

As in every society, the Eritrean people have their own customs & norms related to their cultural & religious beliefs. To see similar events of life get different rite & culture in a common bounden duty is a given phenomenon of the peoples' custom. And it leaves any spectator to wonder among the vast cultural heritage & unity of the people's formalism. From joyous event of a new born baby to the process of life & finally death, societies have their own philosophy & tradition. And Eritreans' tend to enshrine their rich & meaningful custom in every event they enroll as that is the main part of their culture. Such example viewpoints are respecting & understanding life its self. A gift of new life is taken very rejoicing blessing. That's why the etymology of a new born baby is derived from either memorial or gratitude of the past or a wish for the future. Religiously, Islamic way of naming a child took place in the 7th day after the birth of the child & it took 40 days for a baby boy or 80 days for a baby girl to have a baptism ceremony in a Christian Religious procedure.

Other important aspect is that Eritreans believe home learning cultural heritage & the accumulation of fundamental knowledge provided by family is crucial for growth & stability of a community. And In Consideration of early education makes a person more reliable, most Ethnic groups join boys of age 10 & above on the conversation of their elders willingly to acquire important manners of once culture & the same goes for girls to their mothers. This old traditional method is being in use for transforming wisdom & knowledge from the elders to the youth & it starts from the early age. It's also a way of shaping a person in to an appropriate, responsible member of his/her community towards his/her cultural & social values.

A society can be defined widely by the festivities they held & a common to all is, the wedding ceremony. As for all people in the world, Wedding festivities are the happiest mode for Eritreans & it's held by gathering all their neighbors & blood relatives, inviting to share the happiness among themselves equally. And also, as it's a joyous moment, they use it for a reconciliation for any past grudges. In Most cases,weddings are similar on their nature of treat with the food & cultural entertainment but the ceremonies held for a religious person may vary on it's norms such as the music is replaced by hymns with chorus & the clothing is purely traditional & religious.

Life's end has an extra meaning & lamentation is not taken only as a duty of the single mourner family. The close community, relatives & friends are also part of the megrims. Due to the decomposing nature of corpse & religious doctrines, Interment rites are held fast,with in a day in most cases, after a person passed away. Accompanied by divers people of family members & friends, the obsequies is mostly effectuate in the deceased derivation villages' cemetery. This differs for Muslims who carry it out in their close-by regional cemeteries & if the deceased is a Patriot, it takes place in the nearest Regional Martyrs cemetery.

Generally, the people of Eritrean is naturally interactive, guest welcomer & has a quality of supportive habits to each other with a tendency of respecting elders & cherishing teenagers. A diligent attitude of working & creativity is a core identity of the society.

RELIGION

In Eritrea, there are four official religions. The Coptic Orthodox, the Islam, the Roman Catholic, & the Protestant. They have been adopted by the people in different situation and their History of arrival is unique from each other. And ever since, the Eritrean people tend to respect and follow the doctrines they enroll as religion is their core value & the people are interconnected with it in their daily life very attentively. The best places to experience them is to visit the worshiping places they use. The church's, the Mosques are open & by respecting to the religious culture they use in the places, they are welcoming to anyone.

Traditional Saho clothing

Bilen bridegroom outfit

Tigre bridegroom outfit

Traditional Tigrigna clothing

CLOTHING

In Eritrea, the clothing culture is different among the Ethnic groups & of course on it's style between men & women. Yet they have the same features of wearing similar colors & meet in the aspect of covering the whole body of the beholder. Derived from this culture, even the modern clothing outfits are not too far influenced by the global trends. Prepared with the innovative new designs of mixing tradition with modern styles that comforts People to wear more traditionally & stylish at the same time.

What's unique is the Religious clothing styles. It differs accordingly to the Religious doctrine they follow & they are normally noticeable. A Muslim women can wear a black rode even cover their faces with it as in any Muslim country is practiced & a Catholic Nun is recognized by the white gown with a covering to the head. In men, although there is similarity of wearing a white gown among the priest of Christianity & a sheikh of Islam. But they can be differentiated by simply seeing in to their styles of the gown they wear. Mostly priests wear shorter gown & also have a chain with a Cross in their neck & their turban must be of white rag.

GEOGRAPHICAL MILIEUS

RURAL AREAS

In Eritrea there are plenty of areas which are outside the boundaries of the cities. They have less number of settlements, low density of population with extremely less noise & air pollution. Nature is more accessible due to the beauty of the farm lands with their domestic & wild life. They offer beautiful landscape attraction by their fresh vegetation, plantations & water bodies.

Rural Area of Embatkala

URBAN AREAS

Asmera, Keren, Massawa & Decemhare etc, are developing cities although comparatively they have dense population & large number of housing settlements. They provide all the basic services to their communities & they are not much affected by air or noise pollutions. They are also home to historic manmade attraction like parks, museums, artistic products & special Art deco architectural designs built by different colonizers in different times.

Asmera the populated city

ISLANDS

The 360 Eritrean Islands are one of the Tourism attraction sites due to their breathtaking beauty of land surrounded by water, refreshing breezes, and tranquil environment. Specially the Dahlak kebir & Green island are well known for their historic belongings. With the help of the authority, they are equipped for hosting guests and also provide snorkeling & diving experiences to feel the deep aquatic beauty.

|12

Around Dessie Island

MOUNTAINOUS AREAS

As the landscape of Eritreas' is dominated by extension of terrain in the highlands and ascending on the East to the coastal desert plain, on the Northwest to the hilly terrain & on the Southwest to flat-to-rolling plains, the mountains are indisputable touring potential for tourists of all categories. They aren't as suitable settlements as the other places & they are challenging & difficult to access. Travelers like them though, as they are adventurous for sports like climbing, hiking & Glider.

SEMI DESERT AREAS

Though it's not much, there is a semi desert places in the Eastern lowlands cloth to the coastal places of the Southern & Northern Red Sea regions. The famous Danakil depression is known for its natural landscape of Sand, volcano, dune, serenity, clean air, Flora & fauna and awesome view of night sky. It's one of the hottest locations compared even world wide but it's also a suitable place for activities such as Camel trekking & camping as they are the herd of the places. They also offer engagement with the unique local culture of the Afar & Rashayda people.

Mountainous places of Arbe Rebuu

Dessie Island

COASTS AND BEACHES

The Eritrean Coastal areas are highly admirable & amiable due to its unpolluted environment with it's fresh & exotic sea food luxury. The Gorgusum beaches in Massawa, the beaches of Gelalo in the Gelalo beach Hotel and the Safirai beach in the city of Assab can be named. This coastal areas also provide an opportunity to see the Marine life in their habitats. People choose those places mainly for fishing & using the aquatic resources for trade & tourism.

Small Ports in Massawa

Coastal lines

CLIMATES

The climate of Eritrea offers different seasons at a time for travelers' experience due to it unique terrain. The usual four seasons are not merely classified a hot season as a hot one or a cold season as it is. At a time, a suitable climates of a place at the high escarpment at once & opposite climate in Eastern & Western lowland places is taken for granted. So the beauty comes on the possibility of changing one's favorable climate in just hours.

Taking this in consideration, It's possible to visit anytime of the year & one can find February to May the ideal time of visit due to the normal suitable climate all over the Nation and in July to September due to the common Summer time visitation of Diasporas' from all over the world.

June to August is a rainy season in the high lands while hot & torrid in the Eastern & Western low lands.

December & January are the coldest months with foggy climate almost all over the nation.

BIODIVERSITY

Eritrea, considering it's geographical Sub-Saharan location, is a biodiverse country, specially with plants & some more than 540 bird species. Through the intensive work of vegetation, plantations, strict care & protection for the environment, the country has made a tremendous progress on saving forests & restoring it's habits. Throughout the past 200-300 year, researches had been conducted by different national & foreigner scientists only to get them excited with new findings & a need for further studies.

The last 100 years till late 1990, were the most distractive era for biodiversity. The consecutive wars devitalize it's content aggressively. And not long

after the National Independence, new National biodiversity policy & Action plan for it's restoration were introduced. As a result the lands are again filled with many plant species & insects. Forests & wetlands have become home to many mammals, reptiles & amphibians.
The Red Sea coastal lines also possesses countless land & aquatic special species.

Fl'fl Selemuna Forestry

RED SEA & THE COASTAL LINE

As a link between the Mediterranean and the Indian ocean and passage between north-east Africa and south west Asia, Red sea is an important trade route between Nations of the world. Its name is derived from the blue alga which, when it dies, turns in to red, Trichodesmium erythraeum. The Red Sea compiles modern working ports such as Suez, Yanbu, Jeddah, Hodeidah, Al-Mukha, Port Sudan, Massawa and Assab.

Perhaps the most ancient of this Ports is the Port of Massawa. From a Maritime viewpoint, it's undoubtedly the finest & by reputation it's known as the Pearl of the Red Sea. As the archaeological findings & the noted History indicates, the History of the Red Sea is vividly emphasized Frequent times. During the 7th millennium BC with Punts & their civilization. The appearance of Ship fleets of King Solomon (970-931 BC) in quest of gold, gems and rare essences from a gold-laden Land. The commercial role of Adulis at its peak development (525 AD) with the expansion & interest of the Roman Empire along the Red Sea. The significant importance of the Massawa, Assab & Hirgigo Ports to the Axumite kingdom & the Adulitae, the population of the coastal area at that time, as they were the first landing points on the long trade route. This historical recordings indicates the huge

importance of Red Sea in connecting the world through out history.

Today, the importance of the Red Sea for Eritrea reminds greater as ever. In addition to the contribution of fishing to the local diet, import - export platform & a tourism milieu with it's extended 1151Km mainland & 1083Km islanding sandy-white beaches, it's also an unpolluted & ready to be explored Marine environment. Its one of a kind as it could be a place of new findings of fabulous aquatic surprises.

ARCHAEOLOGICAL SITES

The understanding of archaeological History to a society is Vital as it's the roots of their cultural differentiation & brings social unity through the historical identity it brought with it.

Indicating archaeology of Eritrea, it's more connected with the Egyptian and the Axumite Kingdoms for it has a main reason of similarity to the Sub-Saharan sites. Eritrea has a rich cultural and Natural archaeological heritage of pre-historical times for it has bold footprints of social, political & cultural monuments as its treasure. Such are Qohaito: Metera: Tekonda: Keskese: Adulis: & many more.

METERA

This Archaeological site called Metera, 1Km to the South from Senafe which has antiquity sign of old City & a structure of old buildings with statues. The famous one, a 2.5m long, is "the statue of Metera" with it's Sun & half moon symbols which indicates the times before Christianity & the old Geez calligraphy words of the people. They used them to thank their God's & ancestors in the name of their Kings.

QOHAITO

This city is can be located currently in Adi khieh, Southern Zoba debub. As many scholars & writers explained it, this rich ancient city is a three days on foot from the ancient Portal city Adulis for it's known as a famous market specially with the trade of Tusk and gems.

The city had a reputation of connecting the trade between the Red Sea &

Metera statue

cities located in the horn of Africa. It's citizens had High income due to the vast amount of the taxes they receive from foreigners & as it's results they were building chateaus for themselves. The city still has the remnants of the structural roads once used to own in it's roughly estimated 8Km diameter in addition to the four shrine-alike buildings which one of them still preserve 12 marmoreal pillars.

The old city's water reservoir, was used to Supply the society's water needs and still it's providing it's service for the current people who lives around the place.

In the place, a rugged underground Caves of Egyptian cemetery can also be found. It were used as a place for mummified corpse of the times.

Overall, the old City Qohaito's remnant indicates that the city was so sprouted close before BC with it's colonies Tokonda; Keskese & Hishmelet for they have similar trends of building structure & they are all taken for the center of civilization along with Economical & political roots of the current state of Eritrea.

Mariam De'arit in keren

ADULIS

This ancient Port City is located in East 39°-40° & North 15°, in the Gulf of Zula, 55Km to the South of the current Portal city of Massawa. It owns a hot climate, specially in the months of June to July it reach as high as 55°C or 131°F. Archaeologist estimate that the city was found in the 6th century B.C. and were used as a link of the region with the Egyptians, the Romans, the Arabs and even with the far East colonies. As the disinterment by many archaeological practitioners encountered, the city was a Center for trade, socio-political affairs, exchange of technological tool and other important interest of the Era. Although it is totally destroyed & forgotten now, Adulis was very famous and spouted significantly in the 3rd, 4th & 7th A.D.

Top view of one Adulis housing

The old city Adulis

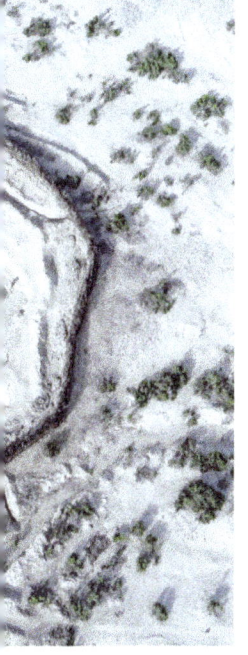

Old Turkish building remnants

THE DAHLAK ARCHEPELAGO

The Dahlak Archepelago has an amazing suitable Hot climate along with natural maritime gifts, Coral reefs with a special diving spot, Sunken ships, different & unique for the place types of fishes. The reminants of cultural monument preserved makes the place additionally more attractive beside the caves of water reservoir which was built to solve the scarcity of water supply of the native Muslim residents of the place as their footprint is left with the Arabic calligraphic passage which still holds bold memory in the cemetery they used. They are part of the Islands count to be more than 360 in number & others are very interesting. out of them, the "Dahlak kebir" & "Nora" are the biggest in size of all.

Sahaba Mosque

MONASTERIES

In Eritrea, there are around 22 famous Monasteries and most of them are located in the high hills of the high lands. Although most of them are easily approachable & some of them only approves Male Gender entrance due to religious reason. They all have adventurous, full of story sites & are all the best Makers and keepers of the "Brana manuscript" the medieval books, stored for centuries. The Brana books are made up of total lather paper leaf & covers. The alignment of the words, the two or three types of inks used in them & printing every single word by hand is their specialty.

Nafasit roads view from debre bizen

DEBRE BIZEN

Its placed in a very high hills & it's impossible to go with cars so you must find your way to the place on foot after climbing a strong inclination for at least 7Km. The founder of Debre Bizen is a Monk named Saint Filipos (Abune Filipos) & the monastery is named after him. It's located in the back hill of Nefasit, a small city 25Km to the East of Asmera. The monastery has a specialty of recording every visitor's Name as their guest of honor & thousands names of previous visitors can be found. Besides it is known for preserving over 1000 medieval religious & historical brana books.

Pick housing of Debre bizen

DEBRE SINA

17Km to the North East of Ela-berid and 30Km from Keren, there is a Monastery & a Holy shrine of St. Mary, in Tigrigna called Debre Sina. It's believed that Josef, St. Mary & baby Jesus has stayed for a little some time during their travel from Israel to Egypt. The place is full of religious historical details & it's one of the oldest Monasteries of Christianity around the Region. It can be visited any time & everyone is welcome to the place.

Debre Hum in Zoba debub

Gedam Tsada Emba

ART

Art was a common culture in Eritrean society since ancient times. The primitive native people who lived in Eritrea had their own way of painting and were using it to record the message they want to show. Like the Qohaito's "Slum beati (ornate cave)" reflects, it was part of the society ever since the old times, with the paintings of animal husbandry of the times.

THE BYZANTINE ART

Byzantine arts are one of the ancient arts of the world history. It is a name for the artistic products of the Eastern Roman Empire. It consists architecture, Mosaic Arts, Mosaic sculpture from Tusk & Fine arts. From those, the painting art is the most common and still widely available art style in Eritrea. The art finds its way to be introduced to the people of Eritrea in the 4th century by Syrian & Egyptian monks. It's mostly available in churches and the direct use of the paintings by Christianity followers results the improvement and need of the art till this day. Many churches still preserve old age Byzantine art and they are the places to find them.

MODERN ARTS

Nowadays, there are many types of painting arts by different national artists and they are available in different places. Different styles like Realism, Mixed media, Printmaking, Pop Art can be named. The best places to admire the arts collectively is the Art Gallery shop & The National Museum.

The visual art Sculpture is also widely available art in Eritrea. Although there are many distinct styles, the free-standing sculpture, partially attached in the base but not to any other surface, such as the statue of Alexander Pushkin and statue of Honorary Idris Awate in gergera dum & the relief style, which are at least partly attached to a background surface are the very common once. Examples of the relief style are the sculptures we usually find in the Art Deco buildings.

Statue of Alexander Pushkin

LITERATURE

In Eritrea, Literature has a long history though it has its own way of defining it self. The knowledge of it has been seen vital since old times. It had much history of it as a traditional poetic form "The Masse". It had been used in every aspect of people's lives. In weddings, Funerals, court gatherings and other special occasion were very common to use it & express the ongoing activities by it. The person who own & Narrate a Masse is called "Massegna" and they earn great respect of their community. They had a responsibility of defining the current situations' of their community in a very systematic way so that the community would get a common understanding of the issue. Although the etymology of the art differs among the Ethnic groups, they were well practiced by the Tigrigna, Tigre, Saho & others.

POETRY

It's known that the last Hundred years were the times of revolution for Literature in Eritrea. Modern Poet's were born & introducing the written form of recording boosted their careers. Specially in the times of the armed struggle, through it's Poetic powerful attraction,it was a very useful tool to unite the fighters for the National common cause.
Nowadays, There are so many Poets and Poetic products as ever and they played a big roll in advancing the linguistic use of one's own language & forms a better understanding of the society.

THE NATIONAL MUSEUM OF ERITREA

The national museum of Eritrea is an institution for a proper presentation of the nations' history. It is located in Asmera & was officially inaugurated in January 1, 1992 by one of Eritrean iconic figures, Ato Weldeab Weldenariam. Since then, the Museum acts on keeping & preserving the Eritrean National heritage as well as studying & presenting historical events & locations to local & foreigner exhibitors.

The Museum has been relocated to a better place to where it is currently located. And it has a branch in the city of Massawa opened in 2002. This Museum, added current & long time maritime monument besides the historical persevered times. Generally the Museums consists of different sections & the main displays are the display that consists of Paleontological sections of evolutionary development and reconstruction of ecological & climate changes in the past millennia. Another section with consists of Cultural development of pre-historical, proto-historic Archaeological records which yields the complex society of the people in the horn of Africa. A section of wild life of extinct & extant species in Eritrea. The section of artistic, traditional & armed struggle history of Eritrean society. The section which Exhibits the medieval times & its impact on the Eritrean society through Religious introductions. And the last section, An ethnographic section with cultural & linguistic presentation of contemporary Eritrean society.

Locumative Lotterina standing in Forrovia

ITINERARY RAILROAD TOUR TO MASSAWA

The revolution of the Railway transportation started in the early 19th century & it had a significant impact on the livelihood of the times. Eritrea was one of the African nations to experience this revolutionary industry in the start of the 20th century. The Eritrean railroad was made possible by Italian Engineers & devoted Eritrean labor workers. It was extended from the Portal city of Massawa to Asmera, keren, Aqurdet & Bisha to cover a distance of 410 km. Although the currently working section of it, is from Massawa to Asmera, it's legacy is still there.

One of the specialties of the Eritrean Rail way is its lasting duration & history. Although it had been made by the Italian colonizers mainly to enhance their dream of making Eritrea their industrial center in East Africa, The sophistication of it's infrastructure is the most amazing part of it. It gives you a clear image of the blood & sweat it took to achieve its completion. Touring from Asmera to Massawa, the exploration through the 30 tunnels & passing 35 bridges with the magnificent view of hilly adventure, narrates a special artifice of the time.

Another specialty is experiencing the four types of locomotives. The steam engined locomotive from the 1930s, the Lotorina from the 1940s, the white colored diesel engined from the 1950s & the Orals which was manufactured in Eritrea. Due to the day-to-day services provided, they all serve as new as they were. Adding to the peculiarities, With in 117 km, the average gradient is 2394 meters, which is very rare in the world. And at its peak from Ghinda to Asmera, it reaches up to 3.5m.

And the most amazing part of it is, when the old fashion horns blow up while the enjoyment you get from the views of the landscapes conceded, with the special experience you get to enjoy of the attractive mountainous adventure from Asmera to Nefasit then Embatkala, Ghindae, Dengolo, Gahtielay & all the way to Massawa.

Marathon athletes Zersenay & Ghirmay leading a competition

Eritrean cyclist winning Continental championship

SPORT

As in many societies, the practice of sports in Eritrea has a long traditional history. Physical sports such as shakie (a cricket-like game) & Hulko were very popular cultural games. And also some non-physical sports like Qarsa, Gebeta, Aderaras were among the common, though they are not usual in current times.

The dimensions of sports were changing from time to time but mainly with the arrival of the Italian colonizers, it's has changed so much. The introduction of Cars & bicycles for the first time gave new perspective on a mechanical sports. On the time, It had made Eritrea the very first place to have a car racing & cycling tournament of all African nations.

Hulko traditional men sport

Along this, ball games such as football, volleyball, basketball and others didn't take that long to be famous around the main cities. And it continues to be that way, adding many more different types of sportive games till now. As it's result Eritrean Athletes won several world Marathon medals & hold New world record on it. Cyclists participated & put themselves in podiums of world stage cycling tournament like Tour dé France, Volta Spaña, Jiro de Italia and other Olympic games.

Though Athletics, cycling, Volleyball, Basketball & Football are among the adored sports currently, many more sports are held in different seasons. Swimming, Boxing, Body Building championship, Ground Tennis & Badminton are some of them.

Fitlee traditional woman sport

Cars & motor cycle racing in Bahti meskerem

MUSIC & MUSICAL INSTRUMENTS

In every society, music is one of the momentous part of the culture. It has made tremendous contributions on bringing the society together by creating entertainment & carrying messages of their history to the future generations & it also plays a key role in ceremonies such as weddings, festivities & religious rituals. In Eritrea, there is a unique practitioner of music which represents the very pure tradition of the people & defining each individual Ethnic groups' culture & history with it. Although using percussions is mostly common to all, the other musical instruments classification such as strings, woodwinds & brass are traditionally available. There are plenty types of modern music and instruments. The traditional ones are very unique to other societies given to their structure & the sounds they make. The musical school located in Barjima Asmera is the best place to visit & experience the traditional & modern musical instruments.

DRUM

Percussions are the most common & basic musical instruments for all Ethnic groups. Although ethnic groups have their own tempo of using it, most of the drums are similar in shape & usage. They either get played in a sitting mode due to their purpose of using only one side, heavyweight or inconvenient shape for a standing position.

Traditional Tigrigna dance

Kirar of Nara

STRINGS

Kirar:- It's one of Eritreas' traditional, string class, musical instrument known for its mellifluous sounds. It has commonly five strings, though in Recent years six & seven strings have been introduced. New design improvement has also been done on Kirar making it produce major & minor sounds which makes it cope with the modern musical trend. Kirar is a common musical instrument in Tigrigna, Tigre & Bidawyet Ethnic groups.

Abangala:- Abangala is also a unique string traditional musical instrument of the Kunama Ethnic group. It's played by using only the two strings of it.

Wata:- Wata is another string musical instrument for the Tigrigna Ethnic group. It has much similarity of sound with violin but it has only one string.

Playing Wata

Emblta Musical instrument

THE WOODWINDS & BRASS

The **Melekhet, Flute & Embilta** are some examples of the traditional instruments. They produce their sounds by sympathetic vibration of air in a tubular resonator in sympathy with the vibration of the player's lips.

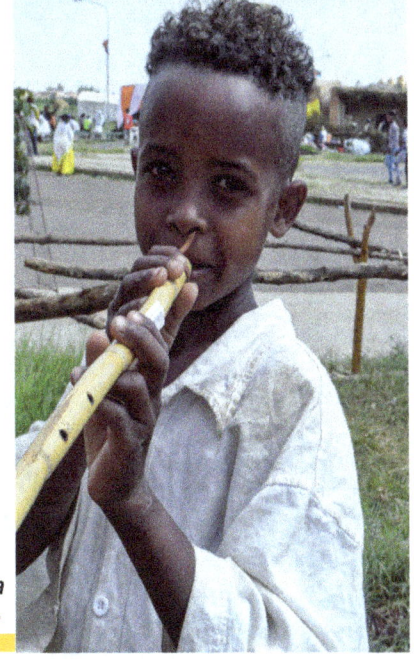

A Tigrigna child playing flute

DANCE

Dancing is a highly valued & acknowledged part of the Eritrean culture. Each Ethnic group has their own dancing choreographical procedures, expressing the purpose & message needed to be carried & transmitted by it. Although using half part of the body, which is similar to many African dancing styles is mostly performed by the Kunama Ethnic group, most of them use their whole body steadily. The Afar, Saho & Rashayda can be recognized by their ricocheting act. The Tigrigna, Tigre & Bidawyet also can be similarized by using mostly their upper body, specifically their shoulder. Dancing is mostly practiced at early age & is performed in major events of community such as ceremonies of wedding, festivities & some special events.

Bilen dancing mode

Tigrigna & Saho enjoying themselves by Gayla

Traditional dancing of Bidawyet

Kunama dancing

Nara dancing style

Fiat Tagliero

TOUR TO ASMERA

Asmera, a beauty as a capital, is located on the highlands, 2400m above sea level which makes the city the sixth highest in the world. It's home to architectural wonders from the Italian colonial era. It has worn like an European fashioned, elegant dress with full dignity. The tailors were the Italians in the early 20th century & they chose it for it's favorable climate derived from it's location on the edge of the plateau in the highland mountains. It's one of the neatest cities in Africa & agreeably one of a kind. Its Nick name was "Piccolo Roma" which was the dream of the Italians to make second Roma in East Africa.

Start your day early in the morning by experiencing the best enjoyment of watching the sun rise with the stunning sight of Fiat Tagliero. The building completed in 1938, has a futurist architectural style and was designed in the shape of an airplane with a central tower & two 15m concrete wings. It's one of the famous building in Asmera & has been described as "the best example of futurist architecture" in Africa.

Taking a long morning walk, you can get to the beating heart of the city; Marcatto, the market place for food stuff for over 90 years. And if you are

Cinema Roma

Marcatto

interested in other goods, you should visit the near by markets from clothes to electronics & other supplies. Don't miss the Medeber market, which takes place in a caravanserai built a century ago to gather all sorts of good from the neighboring countries.
Now it offers a beautiful Art deco frames with an innovative metal works & goods. Its also a place where red peppers (berbere) are prepared, the mixture of spices typical in Eritrea.

Lovers of espresso must stop at one of the oldest Italian-style coffee shops in the city. Bar tre-stelle offers great coffee & serving along with a pool table. Asmera Sweet cafe & Cinema Roma cafe can also provide alternative espressos. If you want to venture beyond the city center, drive along the red unasphalted roads, which contrast beautifully with the green eucalyptus - as far as the popular districts of HazHaz & Mihramchira. From the top of their hills you can enjoy one of the widest panoramic views of the city. Located near the Mieda Eritrea bus station, Enda Mariam Orthodox Church is dedicated to St. Mary; a unique blend of Habesha & Italian architecture. A very special occasion not to be missed is a weekends wedding ceremony. Daily the Coptic rites

Medeber

coexist in the city center with the call of the muazzin from the nearby great Mosque of Al khulalfa and the tolling of bells of the Catholic Cathedral Nostra Signors del Rosario.

The tank cemetery, in the suburban area towards Tsetserat is surely worth a visit; it is a home to massive heaps of hundreds of burned tanks in memories of the extended armed struggle along with disused cars, civil buses, vans with Cyrillic inscriptions, is a sort of open air museum of recent history.

You can't miss the evening walk along

Burned & misused Tanks

the main central street of the city ,Harnet Avenues, lined with palms & some of the most impressive & best preserved architecture. Starting from Bahti meskerem to city park then shida square, the avenue is busy with people of all ages. Don't forget to stop in at one of the many street cafes such as Impero, Bar Royal or Portico and enjoying a cappuccino or macchiato beverages.

FESTIVAL

In Eritrea festivities are part of the culture and they are widely practiced by the society. For different occasions, there are plenty of small community gathering & big national festivities.

THE NATIONAL FESTIVAL

The Eritrean national festival is, one of the biggest festival that participate all the Ethnic groups from all over the places. It's yearly festivity held in summer time (in July) & it provides detailed cultural practices of each Ethnic group, different artistic shows, book fair, exhibition, recreational centers and other important artistic shows. It's attended & enjoyed by different group of ages as it provides

Festival Expo entrance gate

interesting content for all. Besides, the presence of all the Ethnic groups with their traditional practices gives everyone the feeling of intimacy to each other. The other side of the National festivity is the one that held among the Eritrean Diasporas in different countries worldwide. The oldest of them is the "BOLOGNA FESTIVAL" started in Italy in 1982 & it's still marvelous in many ways. Following the BOLOGNA, every Eritrean community in any country starts celebrating a festival jointly with the Eritrean Independence Day.

THE N.E.U.Y.S SAWA FESTIVAL

This festival is widely known with its tridimensional participants of current graduates of the Eritrean National Service training program, the MAMOS participants & the Eritrean Diasporas who participate in different national activities. It's a bi-yearly, held in the Medina of youth, in Sawa. It generally shows the achievement of the youth & their tendency to inherit the national purposes.

ERITREA THROUGH OUT THE YEAR

Eritrea uses the standard fiscal year & the first holiday it encounter is the New Year Holiday. The people celebrate New year widely as it's also an international holiday.

LIDET (X-MASS)

A week after New year, on January the 7th, is the ge'ez Christmas. It's celebrated widely among the orthodox Christian followers nation wide. & It's also Eritrean national holiday.

FENKIL

In the 2nd week of February, the days are memorable days for every Eritrean citizen. The days of the Operation Fenkil. It's conducted every year with great enthusiasm in its place of accomplishment, the Portal city of Massawa. With the cold season of the region, almost every visitor wishes to stay for more enjoyment.

INDEPENDENCE DAY

On the 24th May, the Eritrean people celebrate their independence day in a very marvelous way. Nationwide it's the biggest & fanciest holiday of all. It's celebrated by different shows of the day and carnivals in all the cities & among all the society.

BAPTISM

This is also a Christian holiday which represented a baptism ceremony. On it's day, It's a national holiday through out the nation although it get celebrated nationally in the capital, Asmera.

EASTER

Easter is one of the biggest Christian holidays. It's is celebrated after a 55 days of fasting, the fast of **Tsom arbea** (**fast of 40 days**). Its etymology says 40 days of fast but it's without counting weekends. It's has a tremendous meaning for the Christian people & it's well celebrated by having a good way possible.

EID AL FETR

Eid Al fetr is a well celebrated holiday of the Muslim society. It's also an international holiday which is held after a fast of 30 days "Fast of Romodan" it's celebrated widely Nationwide.

MARTYRS DAY

The Eritrean people won their Independence after a long war which takes the life's of many fighters beside the other costs & it continues by all those who die a heroic death on keeping the trusteeship they received from their Martyrs. In 1993, the day 20th June, is set as the Martyrs day in the memories of all those valiants who shed their blood for the people's freedom & prosperity.

ED AL ADHA

This Ed is celebrated after the end of the 10 days of Hajj or Omra, the religious visitation of Muslims to the holy place in ,Mecca Saudi Arabia. Though some people may visit but most of them celebrate it their home country with their families & beloved one's

SEPTEMBER 1ST

September first is the National holiday held for the memory of, the starting day of the armed struggle in 1961. It's well remembered & celebrated by the people as it indicates the starting day of the act for the essential taking back of their suppressed freedom from colonizers.

QUDUS YOHANS

As the orthodox Christian Church use the ge'ez fiscal year, New year starts in September. The ge'ez calendar time line is mostly 8 days & surely 8 months & 8 year back from the international Gregorian calendar. As a result the "Qudus Yohans" holiday is a new day of their New year & It's also a national holiday as the orthodox followers celebrate it very highly.

MESQEL (THE CROSS)

Mesqel also known as Damiera is one of the religious orthodox holidays of the year,it's usually held in August & its for a remembrance of finding the holy Cross after hundreds of years. It's celebrated by religious hymns & liturgy all across the Nation.

THE ROMAN CATHOLIC CHRISTMAS

On 25th December, the Catholic Church of Eritrea celebrates the Christmas holidays. It's an international holiday which makes it well celebrated among the Catholics & others Christian.

CUISINE

Eritrea has an exquisite traditional foods which can be varying in different ways from the rest of the world and they can be recognized as a heritage. Though Western & Arabian foods are widely available, many traditional foods are served & are daily cuisines of most Ethnic groups. And the way of eating food is different due to using hands to eat it & in a gathered way. Eight or less people get combined together to have a common provided foods. This tradition is called a " Meadi". It's common for all Ethnic groups & it's a well respected due to its importance of bringing intimacy among the people.

A mixed dish of all kind

Gogo to be served

- **Taita or injera** :- Taita is a very common traditional baked food which is prepared from Taff, wheat or Corn. It's processed through fermentation and baking in it's one side in a tenuous way.

- **Hanza** :- it's a delicate food which is prepared only from Corn. It goes all the same process as Taita except for it's folded two at one conceded & a little more thicker than Taita.

- **Gogo** :- it's a type of thick unleavened bread, a very nice taste loaf made from barley . A little tough to swallow it is, which makes it breadwinner with a little of it. It's so common in rural areas & it's a free of sugar & baking soda.

- **Tihlo** :- this meal is the same with Ge'at but only differs on the way it got eaten. A Ge'at can be eaten with hand or using spoon & Tihlo is eaten with Single chopstick. And the butter is replaced with Zgni Qanta which makes it delicious in whole.

Ge'at Saho

- **Ge'at** :- this is a very yummy and nutritious food commonly used by all people. It's made with a flour torrided by a very hot water then add butter, yogurt & pepper in a traditional manner while it's served. The flour can be Corn, wheat, or barley and they can give different tastes accordingly.

Shiro

- **Shiro** :- it's a total by-product of chickpeas and it passes so many processes before it's ready to be chowdered. It's very tasty supplimented by spices. And also it is the most common food anywhere.

Preparing sheya

- **Sheya** :-Sheya is a one of Eritrean tasty meal which is served usual around Gash Barka specially in the city of Tesseney. It's a barbequed meat prepared by using a special barbeque method of small smoothie stones, collected from rivers. By placing the stones above an oven in a pattern way leaving no space to spare, the stones get heated in a way they can avoid the unwanted smell which can derive from the fire woods. Finally the meat is stewed in the broiled stones after it gets mixed with the necessary sauces.

- **Hisho** :- it's a traditional meal made with Taff & butter. It's unique preparation makes it very tasty & eating too much is not normally recommended.

- **Kicha-FitFit**:- it's crumbs of unleavened breads which is prepared specially for this meal and this gets mixed with fricassee. This meal is usually served as a breakfast.

- **Qanta** :- it's a name for a starked meat but prepared as a Zgni sauce only it's another tasty version of the Zgni type.

- **Zgni sga** :- it's a type of ragout which can be prepared by white meat, onions, butter, and other essential spices. It also can be prepared with or without pepper as guests choice.

- **Dulot** :- This abdominal parts of herbivorous mammals is well prepared after giving it an extra cleanliness. Adding garlic, chilly sauces & a little fat when its cooked, it results to a yummy special cuisine. People tend to use needed meaty part, of sheeps and goats.

Veggies

- **Ful** :- this type of food is usually being served as a breakfast and though it's prevailing Nationwide, it's a very common to places of the Anseba region & Gash Barka. It's prepared from a previously dried then stewed bean in a high heat for extended hours. After it takes it's easy to digest form, sauces get added as flavoring as needed. Depending on the sauces, there are different varieties of Ful & it's a delicious breakfast meal loved by many.

- **Luhluh** :- Luhluh is one of the types of scone prepared usually from wheat flour. It's etymology is derived from it's thin thickness. With enough experience, it don't take much time to make it by anyone as the flour only needs to be mixed with water & get baked. This scone is very common with the Afar Ethnic group in the coastal Miliues.

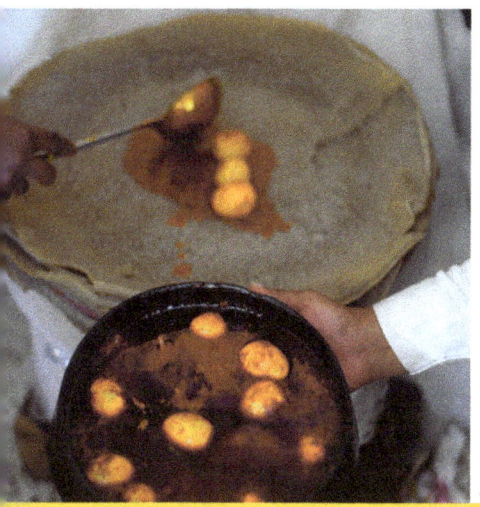

- **Zgni Derho** :- this meal referred as a traditionally prepared chicken ragout. It has its own way of preparing it by bisecting the Chicken into twelve parts & adding twelve stewed eggs while serving it with Taita.

Zgni derho

- **Wieka** :- wieka is a by product of a dried then grinded Okra used as a chowder by it's self or companied with shiro or Zgni, it creates a moisture which gives a good flavor & make the stew more yummy. It's a common food in places of zoba Gash Barka & Anseba. It has high health benefits of preventing constipation.

- **Hilbet** :- is prepared totally from soybean. It gets to be processed in a flour form before it gets torrided by boiling water. Then it will be served mixed with sauce and eaten by injera.

The big cities in Eritrea has many variety of foods available. Different types of fishy meal, different kinds of Pizzas, Burgers and many Arab foods are served by Hotels, Restaurants and most snack-bars.

TRADITIONAL DRINKS

There are plenty of traditional drinks & due to their occasional timing of brewing, they are not easily found. Which is, they are served in special ceremonies & festivities.

Traditional coffee

- **Coffee** :- In many societies, coffee is a usual drink due to its only refreshing impact. But in some places it's different in it's formality. In Eritrea it has its own ceremonial ways. It's more like a chatting mode extended for two or less hours which gathers a whole family or friends to spend a leisure time together. Although the host is usually a woman, it could be a man too, depending on the culture of the Ethnic group i.e. Nara, Tigre, Bidawyet. The needed settings to organize the formality also could be different from place to place i.e. the highlands way needs more accessories. But the copper to the coffee is the same for all, the famous Jebena, a pot like locally made porcelain.

Pouring Swa from it's holder jar

- **Swa** :- Swa is a very common traditional alcoholic drink usually enjoyed in the high lands by the Tigrigna Etnnic group. Its only ingredient is sorghum but it has to be milled, baked, aridded & fermented adding enough water, before it get brewed. Usually woman know it's recipe & do it with great care & It take them about two weeks of processing to get the final brewed product. It has different versions presenting it like Tsiray,

Duqa, Zlil & others. The people use a Pannikin called "Melelikh" as a drinking tool & It's well enjoyed among those who drink it. Finding it would be easy in most tigrigna ceremonies. Due to its unmeasured alcoholic nature, it's recommended not to drink too much of it.

- **Mies** :- It's another traditional alcoholic drink, only it differs on it's strength as the effect of the honey brewed with it. It's such a sweet drink in its test yet strong alcoholic beverage not to take it as easy as Swa. The flask which is used as a drinking tool is called " Birle" & It's served widely while enjoying festivities.

Mies served in Meadi

- **Abaeke** :- It's a non alcoholic drink, common among all the ethnic groups, which brewed from seeds fenugreek. It takes 3 to 4 days to process it & in most cases Sugar is added to make it succulent. Although they are usually available in daily bases, they are famous in Muslim pilgrimages & weddings.

- **Entatie** :- This too is another non alcoholic drink brewed from flax which is usually known for its Satietying ability. It's very useful drink during Farming & other physical activities. It's common among all ethnic groups & it's has also a good health impacts.

- **Daga** :- This is basically a traditional alcoholic drink of the Kunama ethnic group & it's one of the famous drinks around Barentu, a place the kunama society are settling. It's made with sorghum & It's well enjoyed by many people.

- **Duma**:- This is also an alcoholic drink of the Afar ethnic group. It's collected drop by drop from a palm tree. It takes it's etymology from the native name of the tree. Though it's not that famous widely as the others, it's well known in the Southern Red sea region specially in the town of Assab.

SERVICES

HOTEL

Hotels in Eritrea generally offer smaller but very good & opulent rooms with a reasonable prices. Booking can be possible in advance & travel agencies can deliver lower prices than direct asking. In doing so you can save time & energy which shouldn't be wasted contacting each hotel. They also give full service on providing Food & drinks of your demand.

GUEST HOUSES

Guest houses are widely available in the big cities. They serve all but food & drinks. If you can cook for yourself, they can provide you with kitchen choirs & you can make your dish anyway you like. Besides, guest houses are way cheaper than Hotel.

RESTAURANTS

There are so many restaurants which can give totally a good service all around the cities. They are known for traditional foods also they serve international food at a good scale. Commonly, the Arab style dishes & most internationally recognized foods are available.

CAFE

Although Cafes provide full services of what a cafe should offer, they are know for their special macchiato, cappuccino & cakes. Specially in the capital, Asmera. Ginger is also popular with coffee and tea.

HEALTH CARE CENTER

There are of plenty of health care centers all around the Nation. With their well experienced medical professionals, they are effective in providing adequate services in addition to the full medical services they give. The cost is also minimal due to the government funds.

Sunshine Hotel

Expo Hotel

Median Hotel

 Crystal Hotel

 Alba Bistro Bar & Restaurant

Daniel Fast Food

www.ingramcontent.com/pod-product-compliance
Lightning Source LLC
LaVergne TN
LVHW020415070526
838199LV00054B/3625